Sea Splash!

GROOVY TUBE BOOK™

written by **STEPHANIE GRAZIADIO**
and the creative staff at innovativeKids®

illustrated by **RUSSELL BENFANTI**

Line art by Rosanne Kakos-Main
Game by Shereen Gertel Rutman
Conceived, developed, and designed by the creative team
at innovativeKids®.
Copyright © 2000 by innovativeKids®
All rights reserved
Published by innovativeKids®, a division of innovative USA®, Inc.
18 Ann Street, Norwalk, CT 06854
iKids is a registered trademark in Canada and Australia.
ISBN: 978-1-58476-019-1
31 30 29 28 27 26 25 24 23 22 21

Not for individual sale

PHOTO CREDITS
Cover, p. 19 top: Kenneth J. Howard; pp. 4 bottom, 5, 8, 20–21:
Digital Imagery® Copyright 1999 PhotoDisc, Inc.; pp. 4 top,
6 top, 9 top, 9 bottom, 10, 11 bottom, 12, 18, 19 bottom, 20 top,
23 bottom: Corel; pp. 6 bottom, 7, 11 top: Corbis; p. 13 top: Carl
Roessler; pp. 13 bottom, 14–15, 15 right: Woods Hole
Oceanographic Institution; pp. 14, 22, 23 top: Breck Kent; p. 16 top:
Eleanora de Sabata, Innerspace Visions; p. 16 bottom: Renee
DeMartin, West Stock; p. 17 top: John Warden, West Stock;
p. 17 bottom: Tim O'Keefe, West Stock; p. 21 right: Brian Skerry,
National Geographic Society Image Collection

The Blue Planet

When you walk on land, it's hard to believe that water covers most of the Earth. But see the world from far away, and five giant oceans make the Earth look like a blue planet!

These five oceans are all connected. The thousands of different kinds of creatures that live in them could swim right from one ocean to another. Most don't travel that far, though. Most sea creatures live in their own ocean area.

Tropical fish dart around coral reefs. Crabs and lobsters crawl over the sandy bottom. Clams slug along on rubbery feet near shallow shores. Turtles migrate through the waves. Octopus and squid squirt through murky depths.

The oceans hold life-forms as big as whales and as tiny as almost-invisible plankton. The sea is also home to seals and to penguins, which waddle on land but seem to fly through the sea.

Down by the Seashore

The seashore is where the ocean washes onto land. The warm shallow water is a good living place for *crustaceans*—creatures such as crabs and lobsters. The shells they wear are their skeletons. The shore is also a good place for *mollusks* —animals such as clams and oysters. Many mollusks have two hard shells that protect them from burning sun or crashing waves. Starfish also live at the seashore. These "sea stars" have sucker-lined arms that help them move over the seabed and pull apart shellfish for food. Most starfish can regrow a new arm if one breaks off.

Above: A sea otter at rest
Left: A five-armed starfish

Mammals, warm-blooded animals that feed their young with milk, also live near the shore. Sea otters sleep and eat while floating on their backs. A group of otters is called a raft! Otters wrap themselves in kelp, a seaweed, so they don't float away while they nap or eat. Sea otters use their front paws to feel for food.

Manatees, gentle chubby mammals sometimes called "sea cows," also find food by touch. Some manatees have three or four clawlike nails in each flipper, which they use to dig up plants and small sea creatures at night. During the day, they wallow on the seabed and surface now and then for air.

Above: A gentle giant, the manatee

Fin Facts

Crabs move in a funny way—they walk sideways! Some crabs talk to each other by waving or banging their claws; others make noises the way crickets do: by rubbing a leg against their shell. There are 4,500 types of crabs. All have eight legs, and most use their big front claws, called pincers, for fighting and catching food. Watch your toes!

Off Shore Waters

Above: A common, or "saddleback" dolphin

Just offshore, the seawater is full of *plankton*—tiny plants and animals swept along by water currents. These creatures attract little fish, which in turn bring hungry dolphins and sharks looking for dinner.

The dolphin is a mammal and one of the most intelligent of all creatures in the sea. Some dolphins enjoy human contact, leaping out of the water, playing games, or swimming with people. Dolphins have been known to rescue humans in trouble and have been trained to help scientists.

Some people believe dolphins can hear and send thoughts. These sleek creatures breathe through a blowhole and swim by

Right: A fearsome great white shark

6

moving powerful tails up and down. They can live for 25 years.

Great white sharks cannot float. They have no air bladders, as other fish do, so they have to swim all the time to keep from sinking. A great white hunts by "stalking" fish and seals. It sneaks up on its prey from underneath to catch and eat it.

The hammerhead shark has a wide, flat head with eyes and nostrils at either end. This shape helps the shark turn quickly when patrolling for fish. The largest type of hammerhead shark can be dangerous to human divers.

Fin Facts

The right side and the left side of a dolphin's brain work separately, so a dolphin never has to stop swimming. The dolphin's whole brain stays awake for eight hours. Then each half takes turns sleeping for eight hours!

ZZZZZ

Left: An eerie hammerhead shark

Living Coral Reefs

Coral reefs may look like rock. But coral is actually made of tiny living creatures called *polyps* and the little houses thay make. These polyps turn minerals from the sea into a hard substance. Then they use it to build cuplike shelters around themselves. As the polyps grow and multiply, the coral cups link together to form a colony. In time, this colony may become a large coral reef.

Sea horses swim slowly in the warm waters of coral reefs by beating tiny fins on their sides and back. A sea horse can wrap its tail around grasses and seaweeds to anchor itself in place. Most sea horses are small, but some grow to 14 inches!

Left: A sea horse, a kind of pipefish

Thousands of brightly colored fish, such as angelfish and parrot fish, live in the world's coral reefs. Many angelfish have long fins that look like wings. These colorful creatures—some blue, yellow, or striped—are often raised for tropical fish tanks.

Right: A queen angelfish, one of many kinds

The clown fish covers itself with mucus so it can safely hide between the arms of the sea anemone, a creature with stinging tentacles. It might sound gross, but the mucus keeps the clown fish from being hurt by the anemone!

Above: A clown fish near an anemone

Fin Facts

In the sea horse home, the male has the babies! The female sea horse leaves her tiny eggs in the male's pouch; then he carries the eggs around and feeds them until the babies are ready to be born. Sea horses keep the same partners for life, and every morning they do a greeting dance for each other!

The Invisible World

Most creatures that live in the sea have enemies that would like to eat them! To protect themselves, sea animals have learned clever ways to hide. Some become invisible by using camouflage, a way of blending in. The creature matches its shape, colors, or designs to its surroundings. Long, waving fish can be mistaken for ribbons of seaweed. Sponges can look like part of a coral colony.

The butterfly fish confuses its enemies with a stripe that covers the fish's small "real" eye. A big black spot at the other end of the fish also

Above: The camouflaged butterfly fish

looks like an eye. That makes it very tough for an attacker to know which end is which!

Crabs hide by burrowing into the sand. The hermit crab borrows somebody else's home and hides inside an empty mollusk shell. When it grows too big for that house, it finds a bigger shell!

The octopus is the master of disguise. It can change color to match its surroundings and protect itself. The octopus's secret is in small bags of color inside its skin. The octopus stretches those bags to different sizes so its skin will grow lighter or darker.

Above: The changeable octopus
Below: A hermit crab peeking from a borrowed shell

Fin Facts

The see-through shrimp is almost invisible. Now that's camouflage! Another sea creature, the scorpion fish, uses camouflage not to protect itself, but to fool other fish. It hides among sea plants and holds very still until its next meal swims close enough to catch.

Creatures of the Deep

Hundreds of feet below the sea, the ocean gets very murky. Even deeper is a cold area—the dark zone. Creatures living in these depths have developed unusual ways to survive.

The giant squid can grow longer than ten humans—60 feet or more from head to tentacles! No one has ever photographed a giant squid, but pieces of the huge squid have been found in the stomachs of sperm whales. Squids' bullet-shaped bodies are formed for speed. They shoot water out of their body cavity to push them along. Squids can release a cloud of dark ink to confuse enemies.

The angler fish is one odd-looking critter! With big lips and spiky teeth, the angler fish has a special tool for catching food. Attached to its head is a long "fishing line" with a glow-in-the-dark lure. Fish are drawn to the lure, and the angler fish swallows them whole!

Left: An Atlantic oval squid, a distant relative of the giant squid

The mouth of most jelly-fishes hangs down from its bell-like top. The mouth can twist around in every direction to catch its prey. Some jellyfish can turn all colors of the rainbow.

Left: A jellyfish floating in the deep

Fin Facts

Gulper eels have such big, wide mouths, they're sometimes called "umbrella-mouth" eels. The gulper has a tiny brain but a jaw that can be one-quarter the size of its body! Imagine your jaw going from the top of your head to the middle of your chest! Some gulper eels also have a light on the end of the tail that glows and flashes to attract a meal.

Left: An angler fish equipped for fishing

Bottom Dwellers

No sunlight reaches the cold, dark sea floor, so little food exists there. Most of the creatures who dwell at these depths have to hunt in the mud to find parts of fish and plants that drift down from above. Odd forms of crabs and shrimp, huge clams, sea spiders, and tiny lobsters survive that way.

The crab is the scavenger of the seas. As it scuttles along the sea floor, it eats small fish, worms, and the "leftover" prey of larger animals.

Other floor creatures filter particles of food from the water. Some live on bacteria near hot air vents. These vents, called black smokers, have tall chimneys that blast black smoke and water heated deep inside Earth to more than 700 degrees!

Living near ocean vents are some of the weirdest creatures on the ocean bottom—giant tube worms. These

Left: A bottom-dwelling spider crab

worms attach to the sea floor and grow in clusters. Each one has a white stalk with a blood-filled red top through which it breathes. Inside the worm is brown spongy stuff with bacteria that feeds the worm. A tube worm has what look like lips—but no mouth!

Left: A black smoker fuming like a blast furnace

Right: Tube worms of the deepest ocean

600

Fin Facts

Deep sea clams as big as 12 inches across have been found on the sea floor. Another type of giant clam lives in the Red Sea and Pacific Ocean. Its flesh is blue and ruffled at the edge. This clam can grow to be 4 feet wide and weigh 600 pounds. If a giant clam decided to clamp onto your hand, you might not get it back!

Earth's Biggest Buffet

Above: A swordfish with a special hunting weapon

Ocean creatures are part of a giant food chain in which bigger animals eat smaller ones. At the beginning of the chain are tiny plankton. Plankton are eaten by small fish, which are preyed on by bigger fish, which in turn are eaten by larger hunters— swordfish, seals, sharks, and whales. An adult swordfish has no teeth, but it can stab or stun its prey with a long swordlike beak growing out of its upper jaw.

Humpback whales, some of the largest creatures in the sea, do not have teeth either. They eat by sucking in huge amounts of plankton and water through mouth filters called *baleen plates*. To gather enough plankton to fill them up, humpbacks form a "bubble net." The net squeezes a lot of

Left: A humpback whale jumping high and free

plankton into one area. Then the whales swim through the plankton, capturing giant mouthfuls.

Killer whales travel in groups, called pods, of 40 or more family members. Killer whales do not kill or eat people—but they do prey on seals and fish.

Skates and rays feed on worms and fish too, but they also eat crustaceans and clams. Skates and rays glide through the water on flapping fins, which look like wings flying.

Right: A killer whale, also called an orca

Below: A giant ray skimming the sands

Fin Facts

Rays may not be the most beautiful creatures in the sea, but 30 different kinds are really stunning—they produce electricity! One kind, the Atlantic torpedo ray, can grow to be 6 feet long. Electric rays live high on the food chain because they can shock their prey with more than 200 volts—as much as a household appliance! Who's going to mess with that?

On the Move

Many animals travel a long way every year to eat or to breed. This is known as *migration*, one of the greatest mysteries of the sea. Scientists are not sure how animals know what routes to take without a map or directions, even when they've never made the trip before!

The marine turtle glides easily through the water but must surface to take in air through its nostrils. Turtles often travel hundreds of miles to reach the beaches where they will make nests in the sand and lay their eggs. Baby turtles somehow know to head for the sea the minute they hatch. Later, when it's their turn to lay eggs, they will return to the same beach! Some lobsters migrate. Spiny lobsters, found in tropical waters, walk right behind one another in single-file, touching the next in line all the way to their new location!

Left: An olive ridley sea turle

Left: A newborn gray whale calf

Salmon who live in the ocean travel more than 1,000 miles to return to streams where they were born. There, they swim against rushing water to lay eggs, called spawning. Salmon can leap upstream, sometimes 10 feet in the air. They can even leap over small waterfalls!

Huge gray whales migrate farther every year than any other sea creature. Gray whales spend their winters off Mexico. In the spring, they head up to Arctic feeding grounds. This trip is more than 12,000 miles—the distance from New York to California and back again—twice!

Right: A spiny lobster walking across the sea floor

The Ends of the Earth

Ice covers Antarctica, at the South Pole, and the Arctic Ocean, at the North Pole, most of the year. Yet fish and mammals have learned to live in the harsh conditions. Fur, fat, and feathers protect them from the bitter cold. Penguins look funny waddling on the ice. Sometimes they slide on their bellies. Penguins seem more at home under the sea, where they "fly" through the water as easily as other birds fly through the air.

Fur seals don't move well on land. The back flippers of fur seals face backward, so the seals can't use them to "walk" on. They have to wriggle, roll, or slide over land.

Above: Penguins at the edge of icy waters

White beluga whales are small compared to most other whales. They live in the Arctic Ocean, where they feed on bottom-dwelling fish and sea life. Sailors used to call belugas "sea canaries" because they communicate through a series of whistles and clicks that humans can hear. Belugas sometimes jump out of the water and rub their bodies on the Arctic ice. Why? Scientists think this odd behavior is a way of scraping lice off their skin!

Left: A fur seal basking in the cold air

Right: The beluga, with its telltale high forehead

Fin Facts

How in the world do polar fish keep from freezing? Polar cod, winter flounder, icefish, and plunderfish all live in waters well below freezing. No warm woolies keep these sea creatures warm. Instead, they have special proteins in their blood that act as antifreeze! Not as fun as a trip to the tropics, but it works!

Sci-Fi Fish?

Some sea creatures are so strange, they seem as if they belong on another planet. These unusual "wonders of the waves" deserve a place in our Fishy Hall of Fame.

The sea lamprey has a frightening mouth that looks straight out of a science-fiction movie. This eel is a parasite: It lives on the blood and fluids of other fish. The mouth of the lamprey is a sucking disc lined with teeth, which latch on to the prey to feed. Sea lampreys can grow to be 2 feet long.

The horseshoe crab is a "living fossil"—it has been on Earth for millions of years. The larvae of horseshoe crabs look like *trilobites,* ancient spidery creatures. The horseshoe crab is not really a crab—it's more closely related to spiders and scorpions. Wearing a plate of armor, it breathes through gills on its abdomen. The eggs laid on the shore by the horseshoe crabs feed millions of migrating birds each year.

Left: The gaping mouth of a lamprey eel

Many sea creatures behave oddly. The Chinese fish swims vertically! The striped goby sucks sand into its mouth and carries it elsewhere to make a nest. Rare forms of coral near Australia glow in the dark. Some conger eels have bands of teeth, can weigh up to 64 pounds, and can live for more than an hour out of water!

Above: A horseshoe crab ready to lay eggs
Below: A curled-up feather star

The feather star, a relative of the starfish, looks like a fan of feathers. It has 10 to 50 arms with wispy, feather-like tubes. Feather stars curl inward when resting. They spread out when feeding, filtering tiny food from the water around them.

Makin' Waves

Here are some fun things for you to make and do with your sea creatures. First gather scissors, paper, air-drying clay or Play-Doh, a shoebox, blue paint, yarn, tinfoil, a hanger, tape, washable ink, blue juice, and gummy fish.

GO FISH!

Object of game: Catch the most sea creatures to win!

Preparing: Cut 4 pieces of paper into 40 cards (2" x 4"). Find the name label on each sea creature. Print each name on a different card; repeat, to make 2 cards per creature.

Playing: Place the tube creatures before you. Deal four cards facedown to each player. Put the leftover cards in a pile. If a player has a pair of cards, he or she lays them faceup and claims the matching toy. The youngest player goes first, asking one player for a certain card to match one in his own hand. If the other player has it, he or she must give it up. Player 1 lays down the pair and claims that toy creature. If player 2 doesn't have the card, he says "Go fish!" Player 1 takes a card from the pile, and play continues to the right.

SHARK TEETH NECKLACE

Making shark teeth: Real shark teeth are cool, but you can make some to hang around your neck without taking teeth away from a shark. Use air-drying clay or Play-Doh, and mold ten teeth into the shape shown below. Make the top of each tooth rounded and thicker than the pointy bottom.

Stringing the necklace: While the clay is still soft, make a small hole in the top of each tooth. When the clay has dried, thread a cord or shoelace through the holes and tie the loose ends to fit around your neck.

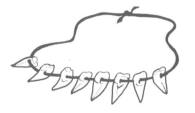

3-D CORAL REEF

Creating coral: You can make your own "coral" out of air-drying clay or Play-Doh. Shape the clay to look like pipe coral, sea fans, and brain coral. Add holes and features with a pencil. When the clay is dry, paint the coral in different bright colors.

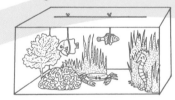

Making a diorama: Paint the inside of a shoebox blue. When it is dry, place your coral in the box with your plastic crab and seahorse. Add grass for seaweed. Now cut a slit in the top of the box. Tie a piece of yarn around each of your plastic tropical fish. Hang the fish through the slit in the top of the box and move them back and forth so they "swim" past the coral!